Poet of The Universe

A Vision of Beauty and Goodness

Dwayne Cole

Parson's Porch Books
www.parsonsporchbooks.com

Poet of The Universe: A Vision of Beauty and Goodness
ISBN: Softcover 978-1-949888-89-8

Poet of The Universe

Faith Poetry

God is the poet of the universe
with tender patience leading
by a vision of truth, beauty, and goodness.
(Alfred N. Whitehead. *Process and Reality*, p. 346).

Dwayne Cole

Dedication

This book is dedicated to the memory of Lewis S. Ford.
While serving as a pastor in Chesapeake, Virginia,
and teaching Greek as an adjust professor
at Old Dominion University, I had the good fortune to meet Lewis.
He introduced me to process philosophy and process theology,
opening the door for me to see new and exciting ways
of understanding God and the world. Lewis' friendship and writings enriched the next 40 years of my ministry. I will always be grateful
for his adventurous vision.

Photo on Cover: The photo of the super moon on the cover
was taken by my good friend, George Wilbur Reid.
He graciously allowed me to use it to show the beauty and expansiveness of the universe.
I took all the photos in the book on my walks and travels in Alaska.

Contents

Introduction

For fifty years I served as a Christian minister.
Laid my sermons on the altar each Sunday
with the prayer that they would
nourish inner consciousness
in a vision of beauty, goodness, and hope.

Retired in 2011,
Became a sermon writer turned poet.
Free to seek more of a union
of science and the humanities
without the religious elephant in the room.

These poems see God in the world and for the world,
in us and for us, acting in saving ways,
setting novel aims and purposes,
and luring us and
all creation toward redemption.

Seeing all things as interconnected,
one in many and many in one,
flux and permanence,
opens the door to faith poetry.

God is the poet of the universe,
with tender patience leading,
by a vision of truth, beauty, and goodness.
(Alfred North Whitehead, *Process and Reality*, p. 346).

The purpose of philosophy and poetry is one—
An adventurous search for truth and beauty
that builds a more civilized society.

My poetry is still a sacrament
Only now I walk a snowy trail
Lay my heart sermon
on a fallen spruce log
with the trees clapping their hands
and the birds singing the anthem.

Bird Song Duels

It is a stupendous fact about nature
that the territorial disputes
of thousands of species
are something like artistic contests-song duels.
The struggle is mainly
musical (counter-singing),
not pugilistic. If only humans
could do so well. (Charles Hartshorne. *Born to Sing*, p. 227)

(This book is a sequel to *Poems Inspired by Process Philosophy*. See the preface and introduction to that book for a more detailed treatment of Process Philosophy. This work is more focused on Process Theology, using biblical images of faith and practice).

Spirt of Wonder

(A poem is never finished; it is only laid aside. I closed my book, *Poems Inspired by Process Philosophy*, with this poem, Spirit of Wonder. I pick it back up, tweak it; and start this book with the same wonder.)

Listen, Spirit of the wild yonder,
as a child on the farm with fingers and toes
planted in the rich loam soil,
my soul was woven in wonder.

As I grew, death came calling
on family and friends.
While still a youth,
encountering grief and sorrow,

wonder slipped
through the crevices of my soul.
A rainbow gone to smash,
shimmering on oil slick streets.

In college and seminary
I searched for you,
Oh, wonder, where are you?
Where are you hiding?

I searched theology books
and philosophical tomes,
highest heavens with angels dancing on pins,
darkest hells with demons wearing pig masks!

With contemplative saints I went into nature.
Be still, oh my soul.
Be still.
Look, Listen, Feel.

I saw fireweed swaying on altar.
Heard birds of paradise singing anthems.
Melodious Mother Nature took me into her arms
lighting a fire.

Goodness blossomed.

Love flamed!
Alpenglow sunrises warmed my spirit.
Kindness of mother moose came to me.
I re-found Wonder.

Felt my soul re-wilded!
Oh, life inspiring, Wonder!

Our Kaleidoscopic World

The Big Bang
Shapes emerge
Colors swirl
Patterns form
Kaleidoscope turns
Planets moons sun spin
Kaleidoscope turns
Plants animals emerge
Humans evolve
Kaleidoscope turns
Darwin synthesizes
Einstein theorizes
Freud analyzes
Kaleidoscope turns
Whitehead physics
and math formulate
Philosophy
Theology
All is relational
Moving from flux
To permanence
Permanence to flux
From force
To persuasion
Unification
Many one
One many
Satisfaction
Zest for change
Actions perish— Yet Live forever!

Poet of the Universe

Conceptual origination
Attained actuality

Poet of the universe
Sharing vision, beauty, goodness

Permanence in flux
Flux in permanence

One perfected in many
Many everlastingly in one

God in the world
The world in God

Tenderly caring Saving all
Light of the world Dawn of eternity

Perishing
Yet living forever

Process Poetry

Begins in wonder
Eternal novel possibilities

God persuasively calls
The world responds

Drops of experience
Entities emerge
Becoming building blocks
Linking like robotic Legos
Making up
the world of nature

God feels the world
Clothing with value

God in the world
God for the world

Relational tenderness
Responding humans emerge

Negation
Positive integration

The many
Unified into one

Satisfaction
It is good

Instrumental goodness
Angels sing

Instrumental evil
Snake looks on with a grin

Forgiveness
Transformation

Reign of God
Reign in God

Glory of God
Ends in Wonder

(This poem first appeared in *Poems Inspired by Process Philosophy*)

Faith Poetry

My religious poetry,
with free awakened spirit,
seeing with Argos eyes,
seeks to create value.

Question the present virtues,
expose the hypocrisy.
The genius of one age
is the enemy of the next.

Just as the sun and moon
illumine the earth
with different colors,
poetry shines in many hues.

Nature writes poems
in the songs of birds,
Aroma of flowers,
bees making honey.

Poetry is more about
how to live in this world
than it is about
how to live in an afterlife.

All we have is this moment—
The here and now.
The present gift—
The world is the poem.

Nature poetry is the spiritual expression
of who we are.
Nature sings the song
of our faith, our being—
The language of our soul.

Einstein described the wondrous
feeling of devotion that comes
from the harmony experienced
in observing nature.

Nature sings the song
of faith, of being—
The language of our soul.

Light We Can not Extinguish

In the beginning God said,
I command light to shine!
And out of chaos light shines.
The light shines in darkness
and the darkness can not
extinguish the light."
The light shines on everything
and everyone coming into the world.
Oh Miraculous Light Eternal!
(Based on Genesis 1:1-3; John 1:1-9).

Part II

We start our lives as a single cell
Divide Grow Multiply.
Molecules swirl
Stitch together
Light glows
Swirls
Lungs form to hold the light
Heart to pump the light
In total darkness the brain spins
Billions and billions of cells coalesce
and life emerges from darkness
Screaming streaming
into brilliant light filled life
Each person formed different
No two snowflakes the same
Air filled light of wonder
At birth we wake to live the light—
What wonders
in this light filled world!

Wonders to behold!
Oh Miraculous Light Eternal!

Part III

Trees born in light
Prehistoric trees
Trees collect air and light
for hundreds of years
Placed in seeds
Air and light buried in ground
Sprout to become light again
and burn bright
Oh Wonders to behold!
Oh Miraculous Light Eternal!

Part IV

I rise early
and walk into the sunrise.
The warm rays
far off yet near
caress my face.
What puzzles there are
in this spinning universe!
Spinning further into Unknown realms.
Yet spinning in our brain
Closed in darkness
Creating miraculous light
Creating rovers on moon and Mars!
Who can understand!
There is wisdom in not knowing.
There is seeing in not seeing.
Purpose comes with clarity!
Light a candle and it always
Points to the heavens.
Turn it upside down
It still reaches for the skies.
Oh Miraculous Light Eternal!

Part V

God saw that the light was good.
Let us live in the light
Share light and life
With each other
Oh Miraculous Light Eternal!

(Based on I John 1:5-7, see my book,
TREES AND DRIFTWOOD: Poetic Ecology,
for an expansion of Part III of this poem).

Victory Over Darkness

Art and poem by my granddaughter, Clara, at age 12.

Life Evolves

As humans evolve from the dark waters,
the Bible promises life
with three score and ten years.

Unless you are Methuselah in Genesis myth,
the grandfather of Noah
who lived 969 blessed years.

Many do not make it to the
magic number, seventy.
You have made par if you reach it.

In God's reckoning
the number seven is
perfection.

On the seventh day
creation was complete.
God said that it was very good.

Adam and Eve
played in the Garden naked.
Became one.

The snake scrolls in the grass.
Flicking his tongue so thin
looking on with a grin!

You know the rest of the story.
Lies and deception sets in—
Sin after sin.

The Garden of Eden
that is where
the Bible begins.

I wonder—
How will it all end?

Why worry?
Get naked.
Play in the Garden!

Being Naked

Adam and Eve, the first romance couple,
You have been placed in many boxes:
    history,
        myth,
            poetry,
                literature,
                    art.

Come out of your boxes
    and become models
        of reconciliation and love.
            Teach us how to live as one.

We are born to love.
    Life's meaning is found
        in loving another person.

Genesis is about a mythic/poetic story of love.
    Adam who was alone in this story,
        found completeness
            in becoming one with Eve.

Adam and Eve,
    the light of myth
        has been extinguished by the church.
            Tell us the truth about love—

We started our relationship
    naked in the Garden of Eden and
        then we got clothed.

You start your relationships
    clothed and then get naked.

Being naked is good.

Mythic Poetry of Genesis

If I could wrap myself in a snowy blanket
and sweep the day under the rug of night
I would not.

There is comfort in knowing
that each ptarmigan feather snowflake is different
even though wafting down they all look the same.

My son, Kevin, says that I morph
into someone totally new every seven years
and why not?

In the mythic poetry of Genesis
God made humans on the sixth day.
Everyone knows that the number six means, hex.

The number six is incomplete,
bumps into seven, the number for complete.
Union of two in sex erases the hex.

Looking at what was evolving
God pronounced that it is good
adding for emphasis, it is very good.

So, after completing six years
I happily morph ever anew
in the seventh,

like a larva into a monarch,
to sip from the honey cup
all over again!

The snake is there
and looks on
with a mischievous grin!

The Meaning of Life

One of the most asked questions around the world—
What is life all about?

We especially ask,
What is the meaning of my suffering?

The questions are so many—
Why did my child die in a school shooting?
Why was my son killed in a terrible war?
Why was my family lost in a car accident?

Why?

As a minister I had to answer these questions.
From the slender threads of broken lives
I tried to weave patterns of meaning.

In asking why
one can find a

How?

Here is the how—
All life is precious, has value,
and holds potential meaning
under any circumstance.

We can not always choose
what life deals to us,
but we can choose our reaction
to what is dealt.

Here is the path of how
leading to healing—

Find someone to
listen,
comfort,
console.

Focus with that person
on the precious moments
you still have.

Center on
goodness,
grace, and love.

If you can not find that person,
go gently into nature
and be still.

Nature will speak to you.
Nature has healing
and restoring powers.

Where is God?

Understanding God!
I am always trying to find God.

What is God like?
What shape?

Where is God, anyway?

The prophet, Isaiah said,
God's thoughts are not our thoughts,
and our ways are not God's ways.

I wake everyday thinking,

Today I will find God.

I see a glorious sunrise,
My soul trembles in awe—

Is this God?

I touch a dimple on my grandchildren's sweet face,
brief smiles as warm as the earth's sun rise—

Is this God?

After driving the grandkids to school
I take a long walk in the Chugach mountains.
Wildflowers and chickadees brighten my way—

Is this God?

I remember Jesus' words:
God cares for the birds of the air
and the flowers of the fields.
God cares for you and me.

All day I walk at the edge of knowing
looking, longing, touching,
in beauty, goodness, and love,

Looking for God.

Maybe I will never know for sure
where God is, but

This day feels like an answer!

One touch of nature's soul
makes us whole—

makes us feel,

In one glorious sunrise we will all heal.

Part II

Safe hunting grounds are not for me.

I often encounter dangerous situations on nature walks—
Mamma bears with cubs are to be avoided,
as are mamma moose with calves.

Hiking in Alaska one can not avoid these dangers.

Theologically and philosophically
some seek safe hunting grounds.

There is comfort in the familiar.

Safe hunting grounds are not for me.
I want to explore new,

and some would say,
dangerous, hunting grounds—

Where courage and logic are required.

Pursuing the devil requires keen eyes.
Having Pascal or Saint Francis as my guide helps!

Heaven's light is a friend and helper.

Who can wait for saintly help and growth?
Sometimes one has to just launch out.

One has to follow one's own calling.
One has to do what one has to do.

Love of truth—
pursuit of heaven's ways has its own rewards.

Babel

Was God really speaking to all persons
when the Bible was spoken in Hebrew and Greek?

Why not Latin, English, German, French,
Spanish, Chinese, Japanese etc.?

Could God not have spoken
a little more clearly?

If I were in charge,
I would have all persons,

animals, birds, etc.
speak one simple understandable language!

But God never asked me
how life should evolve.

Did God ask thee?

Haibun

(literary form originating in Japan,
combines prose and haiku)

On our farm chickens run wild
Loving brown mother hen looks on
Brood of multi-colored chicks with caring eyes
and protective angel wings
Like caregivers everywhere.

Three Haiku (literary form originating in Japan,
Using economy of words. Three short lines.
First line has five syllables, second has seven,
and third has five. Emphasis is on few words
and can have slight variations in syllables.)

white majority
blacks and Hispanics rising
fear runs rampant

Omen of future
brown will dominate culture
in America

color of her brood
sends message to broken world—
love knows no color

Precious Gift of Life

A child is like a dove.
Precious gift from heaven above.

a smile as warm as
the earth's sun rise.

Goes to school
on the wings of hope,

Bang!!! Bang!!! Bang!!!
never comes home again!

Part II

Ringing, reverberating sounds
not the school bell.

More the sounds of hell.
Youth turn the ringing into an alarm bell.

All assault rifles
should be banned.

Collected and melted down.
To make school desks.

Part III

A child is like a dove.
Precious gift from heaven above.

a smile as warm as
the earth's sun rise.

Goes to school
on the wings of hope.

Bang!!! Bang!!! Bang!!!
never comes home again!

Do Not Worry

Jesus said,
Do not worry about your life—

What you will eat or
what you will wear.

Many who heard these words
were poor and without a warm coat.

Was it kind to say to them
don't worry?

I worry some days.

Not about food or clothing,
I have more than enough.

I worry if the rivers will become
too polluted for salmon to return and spawn.

I worry if I will get dementia.

Have a heart attack
or fatal car crash.

I worry if my grandchildren
will be victims of school violence.

I put on my walking clothes.

Go out and hear the birds sing
and sit among the wildflowers.

I hear Jesus say,
God cares for the birds and flowers.

God will care for you.
I join the angelic chorus
and rest in peace.

Kindness Prayer

I want to be kind.
I try hard to be kind.

I would like to say,
"You are fired!"

There!
I've said it.

When Morning breaks,
I will try to be kind.

A Miracle of Love

I often walk snowy nature trails
and ask, what does it all add up to?

Every snowflake different,

The snowshoe hare with puff tail,
hopping across the powdery trail,

The eagle
tipping his white cap,

The ptarmigan with winter plumage
sweeping the spruce limbs with feathery broom.

What does it add up to?

One blessed person's lifetime bio
of joy and delight

from morning
till night.

Or civilization's footprint?

That it is still here all along this snowy trail,
in this winter wonderland,
yet buried in our Pleistocene genes.

Is a miracle of love!

Does God Break the Rules?

Some days it does seem that God
who makes each beautiful day
and meets it with kindness,

also,

breaks the rules and
takes life at will—

Babies who die in the womb.

Children who drown in swollen streams.

Youth by the gang-banger's gun.

Adults with broken dreams.

Some days it is as though God walks
through the flower fields,
and talks—

Don't do this
and don't do that
whacking with a switch
the flowers in their prime!

Leaving us to pick up the bleeding hearts.

Birds and Flowers

Jesus spoke of the birds of the air
and flowers of the field.

Seeing and hearing birds,
the brain makes melodic music.

My heart is thankful
for the graceful beauties

who dance upon the wind
and make the music of the spheres.

Seeing and smelling flowers,
my soul is enraptured.

Cupping the flower,
my spirit breathes,

"Thank you for the grace of your blossoms,
the sweetness of your breath.

For sprinkling heaven's colors,
along my earthly path."

Considering how God cares
for the birds and flowers,

I believe and trust
in God's care for me.

This snowshoe hare visits my yard often. He is rapidly putting on his white fur coat as winter snows are coming soon. I placed the rock in my yard in a way that it would collect warm sun rays.

My furry friend loves to sit on the warm rock when temperatures drop.
I don't know how to define kindness,
but this feels like a step in the right direction.

Kindness Blessing

May kindness be in our thoughts,
making them good and loving.

May kindness be in our eyes,
leading us to see the precious gift of life.

May kindness be in our hands and feet
so that we may be of service to others.

May kindness be in our whole being –
Making us one with God and the universe.

I don't know how to define kindness,
but I know for sure when I feel it.

Kindness is the universal language
expressed in most religions.

Kindness is the language
the deaf can hear and the blind can see.

Peace Dove

How many wars will mar the earth
before the bombs cease?
How many men and women will fall
before the world finds peace?

How many parents will grieve,
holding the folded flag,
painfully caressing the memories,
before the world finds peace?

The answer is in the dove
that comes from heaven above.
The answer is in the dove!

Part II

I had a son who was like a dove
a precious gift from heaven above.

I enjoyed weaving
socks and gloves.

He went to war filled with pride.
Came home in a box without socks.

I caressed those feet
calloused and stained.

I knitted a pair of booties
stained with tears.

Now I am grieving
locked in pain.

Bending the Universe to God's Will

Jesus said
he wanted to bend the universe
to God's will.

Thy will be done
on earth as it is in heaven,
Jesus prayed.

Tweet this message.
Birds sing it to me every day.
They know heaven's way.

I pray that our world leaders
Will learn Jesus' prayer.

God cares for the birds,
God cares for you and me.

My Shepherd (Based on Psalm 23)

When I walk through fields of wildflowers
I know God is my shepherd.

When I wade in gurgling streams filled with wild salmon
God refreshes my faith in goodness.

When I walk through dark Alaska nights,
God is leading me.

God is with me and
I am not afraid.

My fly rod is
a shepherd's rod.

Each cast removes my fear
and makes me feel safe.

Grace fills my cup
until it overflows.

Each day of my life
Kindness and love are with me.

In God's house of nature
I will live forever.

(This poem first appeared in my book,
Down on the Farm in Georgia: A Poetic Memoir,
as an expression of my family's faith in God's kindness.)

Sacred Altar

As I walk in the foothills of the Chugach,
I make a fallen spruce trunk my altar
and offer up all the suffering
of the world as my sacrifice.

The sunlight falls on the altar.
The shadow of young trees become the souls
of all those who yearn for the awakening of a new day
to walk in a safe way.

My prayer at the sacred altar
in the goodness and beauty of nature is this---
God, let the fire of your Spirit lure us,
healing all our ills,

revealing all our wrongs,
showing kindness to the throngs,
drawing all into one family
held in love.

Contemplation of Nature

Contemplation of nature
is the first step
in knowledge of God.

Nature is like a mirror
in which we look
to see the face of God;

Jesus preached the Gospel
not only in word,
but also in images

of birds and flowers,
crops and fields,
Jesus' gentle life spoke

and his kind words acted.
Ordinary words with
extraordinary meaning.

Each spoken and acted word
wrapped in a miracle
of healing kindness.

Whose Story?

As I read in the Gospels about
the gentle life and tender teachings of Jesus,
I ask, whose story is this?

Jesus'
Disciples'
Yours, Mine?

Our lives are written
in Jesus' gentle life and
tender teachings like a gospel map.

A part of the hungry crowd,
miracle bread and fish
received a plenty.

Our stumped toes
on his journeys
in Galilee.

Crown of thorns, scourge of whips.
Nails in his hands and feet,
I feel as my story line.

Easter resurrection
is your story
and mine to tell.

Gentle love teaches me
that in faith stories
we all are one.

(This poem was written, laid aside, and picked back up, growing into my book, *Gentle Galilean Glories: The Tender Teachings of Jesus.)*

A Positive Outlook

I grew up drawing water from a deep well.
It was tiring to think,
No matter how full the bucket came up
it always went back down empty.

Later in life I read a fable
that gave the bucket's perspective---
No matter how empty I go down
I always come back full.

This fable taught me:
The importance of a positive outlook.
Do we face each day
with frowns or smiles?

Do we see the sunrise
as just another
day of surprise
or the opportunity to rise and shine!

The Many Become One

As I walk in nature
I contemplate

How everything is in process
with infinite variation.

I see value in everything
and everyone.

All have great potential for good
and equally great potential for evil.

I feel all things as one
as interconnected and interrelated.

I walk on as heaven
and earth become one.

Without loss of uniqueness
and with the zest of oneness.

Sacrificial Love

In the wilderness of temptation
Jesus chose the role of suffering servant
and not worldly power;
Jesus would not climb to the "pinnacle of the Temple"
to perform a spectacular leap of faith.

Instead,
he would climb Calvary's hill
to dash his life against
an old rugged cross.

The power of his sacrificial service
and love would draw all people to God.

The crowd always wants a God of
powerful and spectacular actions,
but Jesus knew that sacrificial love would be
the real drawing power:

"When I am lifted up from the earth,
I will draw everyone to me (John 12:32).

The wisdom of the ages has proven Jesus right.
People are not won by sham and show,
but by sacrificial love and kindness.

The world needs
not a sign,
but a Savior!

There was a unity
to the life teachings
and the death of Jesus.
His words acted kindness
and his actions spoke kindness!

Jesus summed up all of his teachings in
one great commandment of loving kindness:

> Love the Lord your God with all your heart,
> with all your soul,
> with all your mind,
> and with all your strength. . ..
> Love your neighbor
> as you love yourself.
>
> "This is how we know what love is:
> Christ gave his life for us" (1John 3:16).

Sowing Seeds

A Greek poet wrote, "what didn't you do to bury me---
but you forgot that I was a seed."
Within a few decades this saying
was picked up by Mexicans and stated as a proverb:
"They tried to bury us; but they did not know we were seeds."
A Hispanic woman on tv during the 2017 Women's March
protesting Trump's inauguration used this proverb and said,
"they tried to bury us, but they forgot that we are seeds."
So the word, seeds, has become a generic term,
saying we are all seeds that can sprout
and grow new life and ways of living together.
Thus in this proverb both men and women are seeds for new growth.
Men need to remember that they may provide the seed for biological birth,
but women provide the egg and nurture the fertilized ovum to birth and
new life.
In this global age, we need to join hands and hearts;
and become seeds for growing gardens of love and kindness.
Some of the protest parades had grandmothers, daughters,
and granddaughters marching side by side.
The seeds of love and kindness in the grandchild knows how to wait.

When Mary laid her child,
gently in a manager,
the seeds of the prophets
that had lain dormant
sprouted into new life.
Seeds sown by God, the gardener,
know how to wait.
The end of waiting comes with
each new beginning.
Who knows
what new beginnings
will come in the girls
marching today!
In the right time and place,
each child can grow and
stretch out into the new beginning
meant to be!

Fiery Monster

The great leviathan of Bible stories
leaps from the sea with open mouth
in pursuit of a school of fish.

Its jaws are filled with sharp teeth.
When this monster sneezes
lightning flashes.
Smoke billows from its nostrils.

Sparks and flames
explode from its mouth.
Its eyes glow like coals of fire.
Its blazing breath singes
every thing in sight.

When this fiery monster
leaps from the sea
all cringe in fear.
Hell is licking its chops!

God, without You,
we are doomed.
God help us!
God have mercy on us!

Entering Through the Backdoor

The only way that I can be a
Christian is to enter through the backdoor.

The front-door is guarded
by border patrols.

The name Christ has been centrally blazoned
on the front-door of our theology and creeds.

The name, Jesus, if used at all,
is placed on the backdoor.

The name, Christ, conceals
what the Bible reveals.

The name, Jesus, reveals
what our creeds conceal.

For most the name, Christ,
soars above human suffering.

The name, Jesus, touches down
with kindness.

In the spirit of saints like Mother Theresa,
who when asked,

"How do you minister to the poor each day?"
Replied, "It is Jesus, really."

I choose Jesus
and the backdoor.

Faltering Faith

Faith is fragile and grows old
seeps like stale water
from a cracked porcelain bowl
flows down polluted streams
destroying many dreams
ending in too stormy of a sea
Oh thou, who commanded
the waves to be still
take my hand
be my will
I have adventures still.

D. Cole

Take My Hand

Jesus walked with his disciples
along the Sea of Galilee,
teaching them lessons of faith.
Once he walked on the water,
and invited Peter to take his hand.

We don't have to go to Galilee today
to accept Jesus' hand.
Jesus lives today and walks with us.
He reaches out to us every day,
in every place,
Saying take my hand.

This morning at sunrise
I walked with Jesus
on this golden road.
All the way to heaven—-
gave my angelic loved ones a hug—
and was soon back.

It doesn't take long
to make the trip
In touching moments like this
when heaven and earth
are not separate realities.

Hell is Licking its Chops

Isaac Bashevis Singer said,
"There will be no justice as long as man
will stand with a knife or with a gun
and destroy those who are weaker than he is."

I shot the devil
and he came back
bringing seven more from his demon pack.
I dropped my bombs
blowing the hinges
from the doors of hell
releasing a legion of demons
to walk to and fro
on the earth
wreaking havoc.
This is the nature of vengeance:
it grows with each new occurrence.
And you say—
The only way to stop a bad man with a gun
is a good man with a gun?
Or you stop wars
by building bigger bombs?
I shot the devil and he came back
bringing seven more from his demon pack.
Hell is swallowing
our poor,
our homeless,
our refugees,
and disadvantaged.

Sacred Altar

When tragedy strikes our nation
I seek solace in nature—
Make a fallen spruce trunk my altar
Lift all the suffering as my sacrifice.

God, let the fire fall from heaven
healing all our social ills,
righting all our wrongs,
showing kindness to the throngs.

Make us all one family held in love.

Sunrise expresses something
that is more than human!
D. Cole

Blossom Forth

Night time spooky dreams
Fears grip like the jaws of a vise
and won't let go
Tossing and turning fretfully
Dawn brings warm sunshine

Go and find a place to rest in the beauty of the sunrise
Feel the colors from the edge of rainbows bathing your soul
with goodness, grace, and love.

Lifted into the presence of alpenglow clouds
Aglow with the life-giving sun
Come alive in the radiance
Rest in the grace of the new day
Be free from all anxiety

Become what you never dreamed
For the first time
Burst into new life
Full of freshness and vitality
Now and forever

Why I Sometimes Walk Alone

Consider me not unsocial
if I walk alone
through the tundra,
meandering by the brook.

Each rainbow trout that glistens
catches my attention and
becomes a poem in my book.

The flowers that wave at me
Contain the mystery of the ages
and find their meaning
on my pages.

Each orographic cloud
the mountains write,
lends color in time
to my rhyme.

The birds chirping their melody
become the tune of my songs
And keep me bouncing along.

I walk alone to open my soul,
to sunrises and sunsets,
the immortal truths of nature
that God wants to show
for life here below.

D. Cole

Wild Eagles

Oh the beauty of wild eagles
Strength of Empires

Wild eagle where death lurks
Glides like a lightning bolt

Strikes a raft of ducklings afloat
One taken in taloned claws

Snared by beauty
Golden eyes glinting fire

Emblazoned on shields
Halos of saints

Oh the beauty
of wild eagles!

Seeking Refuge

It is Thanksgiving morning.
Beth and I are at our little cabin
on the banks of Reelfoot Lake,
a State Park and National Wildlife Refuge in western Tennessee.

Reelfoot is a 23,000 acre
wonder of nature
formed by earthquakes starting in December of 1811
and continuing through January of 1812.

The ground along the Mississippi River sank
and the river ran backwards
overflowing its banks
and flooded thousands of acres.

On this Thanksgiving morning, I was awakened
by loud shotgun blast from duck hunters.
Hunting was allowed in some of the privately owned
areas around Reelfoot.

As a lover of ducks,
I cringed when hearing the guns.

The loud shots were soon followed by the squawking
of eagles near our cottage. I looked out from my deck
and saw two grown eagles followed by two juveniles
flying to the large cypress trees around our cottage.

They were frequent visitors, finding safe lodging there in the past.
The guns quieted. I sat quietly drinking my coffee
with the family of eagles
resting overhead.

My deck over the water,
under the large cypress trees,
was a place of rest
and contemplation for me.

I wondered what the eagles,
just 75 feet over my head,
felt as they quietly rested.

Even with their keen hearing and sharp eyes,
they did not hear or see the twin towers
explode from the crash
of the terrorist piloted planes.

And come crumbling down
with humans screaming
and leaping to their death.
Sirens squalling

The eagles did not know
that they were protected
from the guns
of the duck hunters.

They had felt the vibrations
and seen their duck brothers and sisters
fall from the blue sky.
That was enough fright!

Being jolted awake by guns
brought for me the sounds
of planes crashing into buildings
and bombs exploding in the war in the gulf.

TV had brought those images over and over into my den.
I identified with the eagle parents
wanting to get their children
safely away from booming guns.

My cottage was a place of refuge
from a world gone mad.
I was there to meditate on goodness
and plan sermons for Advent and Christmas.

Without warning and without mercy
the gunshots had flung me out of my bed,
tossing me to both sides of our beautiful world,
from New York to Iraq and back.

The same exploding guns had sent the anxious
eagle family flying across Blue Water Basin,
the largest of the Reelfoot lakes,
to the safety on my shore.

The flapping of their wings were large pages of a world atlas
flipping rapidly
revealing our sordid gun filled
and war-torn chapters.

I do not know why they chose my cabin.
Perhaps they had heard me last year
turning the pages and preaching my Advent sermons
to a flock of cormorants on Upper Blue Basin.

Hopefully they found me to be a friend of the birds.
Maybe they had seen me carefully mowing
around the place in my yard where the mother turtle
dug her nest and laid her eggs.

I would like to think that they had heard this Advent gospel:
Let God's love and kindness shine in our war weary world
like the sun that rises in the sky, and guide us
into a life of peace and goodwill for all.

The Shape of Love

(Based on John 3:16)

God
loved
us so Jesus us lives in beauty
much who how our and
that shows to live goodness
God gave us

If eyes are made for seeing
Beauty needs no other
reason for Being
D. Cole

God blesses the heart
that bows
in adoration of beauty
D. Cole

Compassion for Suffering

Haibun

I tenderly care for my bleeding-heart plant,
growing by my condo, as a beautiful reminder
to show compassion
for the suffering of others.

Haiku

Hurting hearts abound
Jesus' heart pierced by a sword
Bleeding for everyone

Praying

As I stand before my bleeding-heart bush,
I think of all the families in churches I served
who sat in the pew lifting their eyes to the cross,
hearts bleeding from loss of a loved one.

I think of all the beautiful persons labeled
LGBT who only want to love and serve others—
Rejected and scorned. Jesus' heart bleeds for them.

Conclusion - Poet of the Universe

God is the poet of the universe
Sharing vision, beauty, goodness

Permanence in flux
Flux in permanence

One in many
Many in one

God in the world
The world in God

Tenderly caring
Saving all

Light of the world
Dawn of eternity

Perishing
Yet living forever

Praise

Praise God for wonderful deeds
too marvelous to understand.

Praise God with dancing
and musical instruments.

Let every living creature
sing praises to God

OTHER BOOKS BY DWAYNE COLE

A Center that Holds: Adventures in Kindness.

A Prayer of Blessing: As You Go Remember This.

A Relational Hermeneutic of Kindness.

A Relational Trinity of Kindness.

BEARS AND MOOSE OF ALASKA: Nature Poetry

Down on the Farm in Georgia: A Poetic Memoir

Gentle Galilean Glories: The Tender Teachings of Jesus

God and Evil: An Ode to Kindness.

Jesus' Transforming Beatitudes: Selected Sermons from Year A.

Jesus' Transforming Love: Selected Sermons from Year B.

Jesus' Transforming Gentle Teachings: Selected Sermons from Year C.

Poems Inspired by Process Philosophy

The Apostles' Creed: A Living Creed for the Living Church.

The Book of Revelation: Jesus' Kindness Transforms Suffering.

The Serenity Prayer: A Pathway to Peace and Happiness.

The Story of the Bible: Authority, Inspiration, Canonization, and Translation.

TREES AND DRIFTWOOD: Poetic Ecology

www.ingramcontent.com/pod-product-compliance
Lightning Source LLC
Chambersburg PA
CBHW040543170726
48295CB00012B/573

* 9 7 8 1 9 4 9 8 8 8 8 9 8 *